IRON AGE

Written by Anita Ganeri

W
FRANKLIN WATTS
LONDON•SYDNEY

Franklin Watts
First published in Great Britain in 2017
by The Watts Publishing Group
Copyright © The Watts Publishing Group, 2017
All rights reserved.

Editor: Sarah Silver
Designer: Matt Lilly
Picture researcher: Diana Morris

ISBN HB 978 1 4451 5304 9
ISBN PB 978 1 4451 5305 6

FSC
www.fsc.org
MIX
Paper from
responsible sources
FSC® C104740

Printed in China

Franklin Watts
An imprint of
Hachette Children's Group
Part of The Watts Publishing Group
Carmelite House
50 Victoria Embankment
London EC4Y 0DZ

An Hachette UK Company
www.hachette.co.uk

www.franklinwatts.co.uk

Contents

What was the Iron Age?

The Iron Age began in around 1200 BCE, when people in Europe learned how to make iron. By around 800 BCE, it had spread to Britain. Until this time, tools and weapons had been made from copper or bronze. Iron was harder and stronger, and was soon being used to make weapons, tools, cooking pots and farm equipment, such as ploughs. It dramatically changed the lives of ordinary people, making vital tasks, such as farming, much easier.

The Celts

The people who lived in Europe and Britain during the Iron Age are known today as the Celts. Although there were many different groups, they spoke similar languages and shared common religious beliefs. Feared for their war-like nature, the Celts were also highly skilled metalworkers and craftsmen.

The Iron Age

Around 1200 BCE	The Iron Age begins in Europe
Around 800	The Iron Age spreads to Britain
500–200	Large hill forts are built in Britain
60–30	Diodorus Siculus writes about the Celts
58–51	The Romans conquer Gaul (France)
55/54	The Romans invade Britain
52	Battle of Alesia – defeat of Vercingetorix
46	Vercingetorix is executed
CE 43	The Romans conquer Britain. The Iron Age in Britain ends
61	Boudica leads a revolt against the Romans

WRITTEN RECORDS

The Celts did not write their history down but we know a lot about them from ancient Greek and Roman texts. For example, Greek historian, Diodorus Siculus, wrote: 'They are very tall, with rippling muscles under clear white skin. Their hair is blond, but not naturally so: they bleach it artificially, washing it in lime and combing it back from their foreheads. They look like wood-demons, their hair thick and shaggy like a horse's mane. Some of them are clean-shaven, but others leave a moustache that covers the whole mouth.'

A modern-day illustration showing how Celtic warriors might have looked.

WRITING HISTORY

Much of what we know about history comes from written accounts and records that have been left behind. Throughout this book, you will find panels asking you to write your own versions of the history you have read. You will find the information you need in the book, but you can also look online and in other books. Use the tips provided, and don't be afraid to let your imagination run wild.

Iron Age life

The Celts were not one single people. They belonged to different groups, or tribes. There were over 30 tribes in Britain by the time the Romans invaded. Each tribe was ruled over by chieftains.

These chieftains came from the highest ranks of Celtic society. Some of the most powerful chieftains were women.

Celtic homes

Many Iron Age people lived in hill forts, surrounded by ditches and walls. These were meant to display power and rank, but were also designed to protect the tribe from enemy attack. Inside a hill fort, families lived in one-roomed roundhouses, with walls made from wattle and daub, and thatched, sloping roofs to allow rain and snow

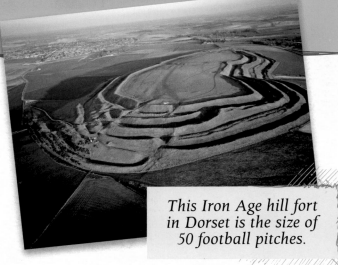

This Iron Age hill fort in Dorset is the size of 50 football pitches.

to run off. Each family had its own roundhouse. The biggest house in the fort belonged to the chieftain.

You can visit this replica Iron Age village in Pembrokeshire, Wales.

Lake living

Some Iron Age homes, called crannogs, were built in lakes or marshes, or on artificial islands. On top of an islands were made from wood and stone. On an island were one or two roundhouses. Other crannogs were wooden roundhouses, supported on huge, wooden piles driven deep into the lake bed. Surrounded by water, crannogs were easy to defend from passing raiders.

Write an estate agent's blurb

You've outgrown your roundhouse and are looking to sell. Try writing an estate agent's blurb for your house. Remember to use lots of persuasive language and to point out the property's best features, such as its location or its newly-thatched roof. Look online or in an estate agent's window to find out how to create your blurb.

Daily life

Most daily life took place in and around the roundhouse. In the middle of the house, a fire burned, day and night, for heating and cooking. Smoke from the fire travelled up through the thatched roof, helping to keep away mice and other pests, and to preserve fish and meat hung from the rafters. Food was cooked in a huge iron pot, hung over the fire. Bread was made by grinding grain flour with a stone quern. The flour was mixed with water, and made into flat loaves that were baked on the fire.

Write an Iron Age recipe

Using the information on the left, write a recipe for Iron Age bread. Start with a list of ingredients you will need, then write step-by-step instructions for making the bread. Look in a cookery book to see how to design your recipe.

Firedogs like this one were placed on either side of the fire.

Jobs and work

Iron Age farmers grew grains and beans, and also kept animals, such as sheep, pigs and cattle. Children helped their parents by watching over the animals, and collecting herbs and other edible plants.

From time to time, some people left the settlement to trade goods, such as woollen cloth, hunting dogs and animal furs, with nearby tribes.

Ploughs were made from wood, with an iron tip on the end to help cut through soil.

Magical metalwork

Some people also worked as carpenters, potters and metalworkers. Metalworkers knew where to find iron ore and how to use fire to turn it into tools, weapons and beautiful jewellery. Their skills were highly valued and even considered to be magical. They were passed on from one generation to the next, but were kept as a closely guarded secret.

Did you know?

At the lowest end of Celtic society were slaves. These were people who had been captured during raids and battles, and brought back in chains. They were put to work on the land or traded for other goods.

Dressed to impress

Celtic men wore tunics, with trousers, belts and cloaks. Women wore dresses, fastened with brooches. For woollen clothes, wool was collected from a sheep, and spun into yarn. The Celts liked brightly-coloured clothes, and the yarn was then dyed, using berries, lichens and bark. Urine was used to fix the dyes. Once dry, the yarn was woven on a loom into boldly-patterned cloth.

Re-enactors dressed in the style of clothes worn by Celtic people..

FASHION REPORT

The Greek writer, Strabo, described the Celts' love of jewellery. He also complains about how vain they were! He wrote:

'They wear ornaments of gold, torcs on their necks, and bracelets on their arms and wrists, while people of high rank wear dyed garments sprinkled with gold. It is this vanity which makes them unbearable in victory, and so completely downcast in defeat.'

Did you know?

Wealthy Celts liked to wear showy jewellery, made from gold or bronze, and highly decorated with beautiful designs. The most famous pieces were large, heavy neck rings, called torcs. These were worn as a sign of high social status, and might be given to great warriors who had fought bravely in battle.

This magnificent gold torc was found in Snettisham, Norfolk.

A letter home

Imagine that you are one of the Roman soldiers who arrived in Britain in CE 43. Write a letter to a friend back home about the Celts you meet and their way of life. The opening of the letter has already been written. Can you use the information in this chapter to write the rest? Remember to tell your friend how you feel about the things you have seen.

Rutupiae (Richborough) Fort
Kent
Britannia (Britain)

Autumn CE 43

Dear Marius,
How are you? Did you have a good time in Gaul? I landed in Britannia a week ago, and what a week it has been. They're a funny lot, these Celts. I was expecting them to be fierce fighters (and they are), but I hadn't a clue about how they lived. Did you know that their houses only have one room, and that they wear loads, and I mean loads, of jewellery?

WRITING HINTS AND TIPS

- An informal letter, like this one, should use chatty, friendly language.
- A formal letter needs a more serious, polite style of writing.
- In a formal letter, you need to include the reader's address as well as your own.
- Find out the different ways of starting and ending formal and informal letters.
- Before you start your letter, make a quick note of what you want to say.

Gods and beliefs

Celtic religion was closely linked to the natural world. The Celts believed that the world around them was filled with magical spirits and supernatural forces.

They considered places, such as springs, lakes and groves of oak trees to be sacred, and this is where they gathered to worship their many gods and goddesses.

Celtic gods

The Dagda

The Dagda was a father-god, linked to farming and crops. He is said to have had control over life and death, the weather and even time itself. He owned a magic club – one end could kill and the other bring the dead back to life – and a magic cauldron which never ran empty.

Brigid

Brigid was the daughter of the Dagda, and goddess of healing, poetry and metalworkers. She married a king and had three sons, who became great warriors. As goddess of poetry, she was said to provide the inspiration for Celtic bards and storytellers (see page 18).

Lugh

God of light, law and the harvest, Lugh was a young, brave warrior who owned several magical weapons. If he put his sword to an enemy's throat, they were forced to tell the truth. This sword could cut through any shield or wall, and its wounds were always fatal.

Cernunnos

Cernunnos is usually shown wearing the antlers of a stag and a large torc. He is often shown sitting cross-legged, surrounded by wild animals, and is believed to have been a Celtic god of fertility, animals and the forest, and lord of hunting.

This image of Cernunnos appears on a silver bowl from Denmark.

Did you know?

The Celts believed in life after death in an Otherworld, where the gods and fairies lived. In Irish mythology, the Otherworld was called *Tír na n'Óg* in Gaelic, the land of eternal youth. It was said to lie far across the sea.

Reaching the magical land of Tír na n'Óg.

Offerings to gods

The Celts believed that sacred places, such as lakes and springs, were meeting points between the world of people and the world of the gods. To thank the gods and ask for their protection, the Celts threw precious objects into the water. Iron Age treasures found in lakes include spears, shields, and even chariots.

This Iron Age shield was found in the River Thames in London.

A book illustration has a druid cutting mistletoe.

MISTLETOE AND MAGIC

In the 1st century CE, the Roman historian, Pliny the Elder, wrote a huge work, called *Natural History*. In it, he describes a religious ceremony, involving the Druids.
'The Druids ... consider nothing more sacred than mistletoe ... and it is gathered with great ceremony. A priest dressed in white climbs the tree, cuts the mistletoe with a golden hook and catches it on a white cloak.'

Bog bodies

Weapons and treasures were not the only things offered to the Celtic gods. There is evidence that humans were also sacrificed. The bodies of Iron Age people have been found in places that were once marshy peat bogs. One of the most famous bodies was found at Lindow Moss in Cheshire, England in 1984.

The Lindow Man was found by peat cutters at Lindow Moss.

Lindow Man may have been sacrificed to the gods.

Known as 'Lindow Man', the man was about 25 years old when he was killed around 2,000 years ago. Chemicals in the peat had preserved his body remarkably well, including his skin and hair.

Write a newsflash

Imagine that you are a reporter, writing a newsflash about the discovery of Lindow Man. Where and when was the body found? What condition was it in? How did experts think the man had been killed? Keep your report quite short but make it exciting.

Festival year

The Celts held festivals to honour the gods, celebrate the changing seasons, and bring members of the tribe together. There were four great festivals in the Celtic year.

Imbolc Date: 1 February

This festival marked the beginning of spring, when the first lambs were born. It was also held in honour of the goddess, Brigid (see page 12). During the festival, milk was poured on the soil, to thank it for the return of spring and new life.

Beltane Date: 1 May

Beltane was a fire festival, held in honour of the god, Bel. It also celebrated the cattle being let out of their winter quarters. Bonfires were built from sacred wood, and people leapt over them for luck. Beltane marked the start of summer and the light half of the year.

Lugnassad Date: 1 August

This summer festival lasted a month, and celebrated the harvest. A good harvest meant that the tribe would be able to survive through winter. Games were held in honour of the god, Lugh, and grains, herbs and fruit, especially bilberries, were collected and dried for winter.

Samhain Date: 1 November

Samhain marked the start of winter and the dark half of the year. It was when the last apples were picked. It was also a time when the dead and the living could move between each other's worlds. The Druids told people's fortunes, and fires were lit to keep evil away.

Write an invitation

You are holding a party to celebrate Beltane. Write an invitation that you can send out to your guests. Remember to include the time and date of the party, and anything you need your guests to bring. You could also add some details of the evening's entertainment.

Entertainment news

Imagine that you are the entertainment reporter for a local Roman paper. You have been sent to cover one of the Celtic festivals and asked to write a report about it. Use plenty of descriptive language to talk about the festival, and why it is celebrated. This will help you to paint a picture for your readers. The opening paragraph has been written for you.

THE DAILY CELT

SOMETIME IN CE 77 ANGLESEY, WALES

BEST BELTANE BONFIRE EVER!

THE LIGHTING OF TWO HUGE BONFIRES LAST NIGHT MARKED THE START OF SUMMER, AND THE BEGINNING OF THE BIGGEST BELTANE CELEBRATIONS EVER SEEN.

'IT WAS BRILLIANT,' A LOCAL WARRIOR TOLD ME, 'ESPECIALLY THE FIRE-LEAPING.' AS USUAL, THE FIRE-LEAPING PROVED THE HIGHLIGHT OF THE EVENING AND THIS YEAR, ONLY TWO PARTICIPANTS WERE DISQUALIFIED WHEN THEIR CLOTHES WENT UP IN FLAMES.

WRITING HINTS AND TIPS

- Begin your report with a catchy headline to draw your reader in.

- The first paragraph should be exciting but not give too much away.

- Interviews with local people will help bring your story to life.

- Explain clearly what is happening – your readers may not know about the festival.

- Look at the entertainment section in a newspaper to get some ideas.

Telling tales

The different Celtic tribes spoke different languages which shared many common words. In Ireland, the Celts spoke a language called Goidelic. In Britain, they spoke a language called Brythonic. In some parts of Ireland, Scotland and Wales, people still speak languages that are based on these. Some Celtic words are also used in modern English, including bog, clan, coracle and even slogan (based on the Celtic word for a battle cry).

The Welsh language is based on a Celtic language.

IRISH ALPHABET

For centuries, the Celts did not write their languages down. The only alphabet we know of dates from around CE 300-600. It is called Ogham, and was used in Ireland. Letters were made up of straight lines. Only a very few examples have been found, carved on stones.

An Ogham stone from Ireland.

Brilliant bards

Although nothing was written down, the Celts loved poems and stories, set to music as songs. They were sung by professional poets, called bards, who travelled from place to place. Bards had to train for many years, learning hundreds of poems, as well as composing new ones. They were highly respected in Celtic society. They could make a king's reputation by singing about his heroic deeds, or destroy it by making fun of his failings.

Did you know?

A bard was given a metal tree branch. The branch had bells on it that rang as the bard entered a place, warning the audience to be quiet and listen. Trainee bards had bronze branches; partly-qualified bards silver, and fully-qualified bards carried a gold branch.

An artist's impression of a travelling bard.

Write a Celtic song

Imagine that you're a Celtic bard. You've been commissioned to write a new poem for a king. Use lots of dramatic language to praise his bravery in battle — it's fine to exaggerate if the facts aren't exciting enough. For a real Celtic feel, set your poem to music.

Celtic myths

Celtic stories told tales of kings, gods, heroes and magical beings. A Welsh myth tells the story of a prince, called Culhwch. He falls in love with the beautiful Olwen, daughter of Ysbaddaden, the giant king. But the giant is fated to die if his daughter gets married so he sets Culhwch a series of impossible tasks to win her hand in marriage. One of these is to cut Ysbaddaden's hair. To do this, he needs to steal scissors, a comb and razor from Twrch Trwyth, a magical boar. Against all the odds, Culhwch completes all of the tasks and marries Olwen.

Did you know?

In the story of Culhwch and Olwen, Culhwch is helped by his cousin, King Arthur, and his knights. No one knows if Arthur actually existed but his character may have been based on a Celtic king who fought the Saxons in the 5th and 6th centuries.

A painting of King Arthur with some of his knights.

Irish hero

One of the heroes of Irish myth is Cuchulain. Said to be the son of the god, Lugh, his magical powers included superhuman strength. In one story, the queen of Connaught tried to steal the famous brown bull of Ulster, leading to war. Single-handedly, Cuchulain fought off the Connaught army using his magic spear, made from the bones of a sea monster.

Cuchulain was given a spear by Scathach, a legendary female warrior.

The voyage of Bran

In another myth, the hero, Bran set sail to find the Otherworld. It was made up of two beautiful islands where people were always happy and never grew old. But the journey was made at a terrible price. When Bran and his men tried to go home, disaster struck. As the men tried to land in Ireland, their bodies turned to dust.

Write a postcard home

Imagine that you are Bran or one of his men, making the journey of a lifetime. Write a postcard home from the Otherworld, describing some of the sights you have seen. You haven't got much space so make your message quite short and snappy.

The Giant's Causeway in Ireland was said to have been built by Finn as a pathway to Scotland.

Tales of Finn

The Irish hero, Finn MacCumhail, was a mythical leader of a band of brave warriors, called the Fianna. One story tells how he tricked the giant, Benandonner, by disguising himself as a baby. Terrified of meeting the baby's father, if the baby was this big, Benandonner quickly changed his mind about fighting Finn, and fled. Read on for another story about Finn.

 ## Finn and the Salmon of Knowledge
*

When Finn was young, he lived with a great bard by a sacred spring. For seven years, the bard had tried to catch the magical salmon of knowledge that lived in the spring. It was said that eating the salmon would bring a person endless knowledge.

One day, the salmon was caught. The bard gave it to Finn to cook but ordered him not to eat any of it. But Finn accidentally burnt his thumb on its skin, and put his thumb in his mouth to cool it. When the bard found out, he gave Finn the fish to eat — for the knowledge must be meant for Finn.

Cartoon strip

Rewrite the story of Finn and the Salmon of Knowledge as a cartoon strip. First, make a list of the key events in the story. This will help you to work out how many picture frames you will need. Each frame should move the action of the story forward.

WRITING HINTS AND TIPS

- Plan your picture frames so that they carry the action along.
- Add speech bubbles to show what the characters are saying.
- Add extra text flashes to help explain the story.
- Text flashes will also help to move the story along.
- Use the pictures and text to tell the story.

War and warriors

During the Iron Age, the different Celtic tribes regularly went to war with each other and, later, the Romans (see pages 26 and 28). The Celts earned a reputation as fearsome fighters, full of bravado and daring. Every fighter wanted to be a hero and claim the glory for themselves. Women fought alongside men, and sometimes went on to become leaders of their tribes.

Warrior world

The Celts used many tactics to scare their enemies. For battle, the Celts painted their bodies with blue warpaint and used lime to turn their hair white and make it stand on end. Most fought naked, though they later wore chainmail shirts. As they charged, they beat their shields, blew war trumpets, screamed battle cries and hurled insults at their opponents.

A re-enactor dressed as as a Celtic warrior, including warpaint.

Weapons and chariots

From an early age, the Celts learned to fight with spears, swords and slingshots. Their weapons were made from the new metal, iron.

They also carried long, oval shields, decorated with beautiful patterns. They charged into battle on chariots or horseback, then leapt to the ground, and fought the enemy hand to hand. Chariots and swords were often buried with great warriors if they were killed.

Did you know?

Celtic warriors cut off the heads of their enemies and kept them as trophies. They hung them from their horses or nailed them to walls. They believed that people's souls were located in their heads, and lived on after death.

Write a battle cry

Try making up your own Celtic battle cry. You can boast about how brave and strong you are, and how weak and feeble your opponents are. The aim is to scare them to death, even before the fighting starts. Then practise shrieking the words at the top of your voice.

Brave warrior

One of the most famous Celtic warriors was Vercingetorix, chief of the Arverni tribe from Gaul (France). In 52 BCE, he led the Celts in a daring revolt against the Romans (see page 28), inflicting a heavy defeat. A few months later, however, Vercingetorix was beaten at the Battle of Alesia, and forced to surrender to save his men. He was taken to Rome where he was paraded through the city in chains. For five years, he was held in prison, and then executed.

A statue of Vercingetorix from Alesia, France.

Write an interview

Write an interview with Vercingetorix after his defeat. Draw up a list of ten questions that you might like to ask him, for example: how does he feel now about the Romans; is he scared about what might happen to him; would he do it all again?

Battle furies

The Celts believed in a blood-curdling group of war goddesses, called battle furies. They appeared in battle to cause mischief and look after the Celtic warriors.

Morrigan

The Morrigan often appeared as a black crow. Before a battle, she could be seen flying above the battlefield. Sometimes, she was seen as a hideous-looking hag, with long, grey hair, hopping about on the points of the army's spears and shields to bring about victory.

Celtic stories tell how the Morrigan foretold death in battle.

Badbhs

The Badbhs were mischievous beings that arrived before battles, bent on spreading fear and confusion. Before one battle, they appeared as three witch-like hags with fearsome blue beards, shrieking victory for the Celts and death to their enemies.

Did you know?

The Irish goddess, Nemhain, was a powerful battle fury who appears in the story of Cuchulain (see page 21). It was said that she could kill a hundred men with a single battle cry, causing them to throw themselves on to their own spears.

27

An illustration showing the Boudica's forces destroying the Roman town of Londinium.

Roman rule

In 55 and 54 BCE, the Romans invaded Britain. They returned in CE 43 and, within a few years, had conquered the south. In CE 61, the Iceni tribe from East Anglia rebelled against the Romans. Led by their queen, Boudica, they attacked the Roman towns of Camulodunum (Colchester) and Londinium (London). As Boudica turned north to attack Verulamium (St Albans), the Romans mustered their forces.

Although they were heavily outnumbered, the Roman forces were better trained than the Celts, and won the bloody battle that followed. Boudica took poison rather than be captured.

BOUDICA PORTRAIT

Writing around 100 years later, the Roman, Cassius Dio, describes Boudica in his epic history of Rome. He says: *'In stature, she was very tall, in appearance most terrifying, in the glance of her eye most fierce, and her voice was harsh; a great mass of the tawniest hair fell to her hips; around her neck was a large, golden necklace, and she wore a tunic of many colours over which a thick cloak was fastened with a brooch.'*

Writing History: Battle Speech

Imagine that you are Boudica. You have arrived at Verulamium and are preparing for battle. Your warriors are tired and hungry. You need to keep their spirits up, so you decide to make a stirring speech. What arguments can you use to persuade them that they need to fight? The start of the speech has been written for you.

Brave warriors, I am talking to you as your queen. Tomorrow, we face the Romans, our sworn enemies. It will not be easy but we must remember our aim. Why are we fighting? We are fighting for our lost freedom and the future of our tribe ...

WRITING HINTS AND TIPS

- Pick out the main points you want to make but not too many.
- Use lots of persuasive language to encourage your warriors.
- Write as you talk to give your speech the personal touch.
- Address your audience directly.
- Use repetition to get important points across.

Glossary

battle fury A Celtic goddess of war who appeared during battle to foretell disaster and death.

causeway A raised road or path across a stretch of water, such as the sea or a lake.

Celts People who lived across northern Europe around 2,000 years ago. They shared the same way of life and beliefs.

chainmail Armour made from small metal rings, linked together to form a mesh.

chieftain The head of a tribe in Iron Age times. Some chieftains were women.

crannog An Iron Age roundhouse built on a raised platform over a lake.

daub A mixture of clay used for making walls.

Druid A religious leader in Iron Age Britain.

fertility Being able to produce young; land that is rich enough to grow crops.

iron ore Rocks that contain iron.

lichen A living thing that is a cross between algae (plants) and fungi.

metalworker People skilled in working with metal and making tools and jewellery.

myth A traditional story that usually involves supernatural beings or events.

Otherworld In Celtic beliefs, a place where a person's soul goes after death.

peat Plants that have rotted down over many years to form soil. Chemicals in the peat help to preserve ancient objects that have been buried.

plough A large farming tool which is pulled across the soil to turn it over, especially before seeds are planted.

quern A stone used to grind grain to make flour.

raider Someone who attacks a place and steals its treasures.

roundhouse A round hut with a thatched roof.

sacred Special to a religion or system of beliefs.

supernatural Linked to forces outside nature or that are not really understood.

thatched Having a roof made from straw or reeds.

torc A necklace made from a piece of thick, twisted metal.

tribe A group of people that have the same way of life and beliefs.

wattle Sticks or reeds woven together to make walls and fences.

Further Information

Websites

www.britishmuseum.org/learning/schools_and_teachers/resources/all_resources/iron_age_people.aspx
Explore the British Museum's collection of Iron Age images.

www.bbc.co.uk/wales/celts
A website about the Celts in Wales, with fun activities from the Iron Age, such as building a hill fort and making a torc.

www.pembrokeshirecoast.org.uk
Plan a visit to Castell Henllys in Pembrokeshire, Wales. It is a reconstructed Iron Age village.

www.bbc.co.uk/history/ancient/british_prehistory/ironage_sites_01.shtml
Visit some of the most famous Iron Age sites in Britain, including many brochs and hill forts.

Books

Horrible Histories: Cut-throat Celts by Terry Deary (Scholastic, 2016)
Britain in the Past: The Iron Age by Moira Butterfield (Franklin Watts, 2015)
A Child's History of Britain: Life in the Stone Age, Bronze Age and Iron Age by Anita Ganeri (Raintree, 2014)

Index

Writing History

Series contents lists

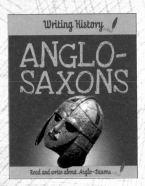

ANGLO-SAXONS
Who were the Anglo-Saxons?
Anglo-Saxon life
Kings and kingdoms
Beliefs and culture
Anglo-Saxons at war
Glossary
Further information
Index

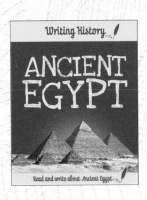

ANCIENT EGYPT
Who were the ancient Egyptians?
Ancient Egyptian life
Pharaohs and wars
Gods and beliefs
Death and the afterlife
Glossary
Further information
Index

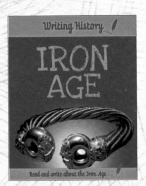

IRON AGE
What was the Iron Age?
Iron Age life
Gods and beliefs
Telling tales
War and warriors
Glossary
Further information
Index

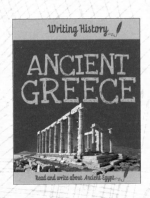

ANCIENT GREECE
Who were the ancient Greeks?
Ancient Greek life
Myths and beliefs
Learning and leisure
Greeks at war
Glossary
Further information
Index

Also in the series:

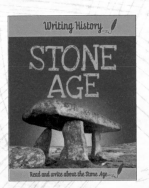